Norman Rockwell

STORYTELLER WITH A BRUSH

Opposite: *God Bless Us, Every One! Saturday Evening Post* cover, December 15, 1934.

Norman Rockwell

STORYTELLER WITH A BRUSH

Beverly Gherman

Atheneum Books for Young Readers

Dedicated to the students at Hillview Middle School, who shared their affection for Norman Rockwell with me.

My gratitude to Linda Szekely, assistant curator at the Norman Rockwell Museum, for many hours of patient searching to find the perfect photographs for our book.

Atheneum Books for Young Readers
An imprint of Simon & Schuster Children's Publishing Division
1230 Avenue of the Americas
New York, New York 10020

Book design by Nina Barnett
The text of this book is set in Goudy Oldstyle BT

Printed in Hong Kong
10 9 8 7 6 5
Library of Congress Cataloging-in-Publication Data
Gherman, Beverly.
Norman Rockwell: storyteller with a brush / by Beverly Gherman.—1st ed.
p. cm.
Includes bibliographical references and index.
Summary: Describes the life and work of the popular American artist who depicted
both traditional and contemporary subjects, including children, family scenes,
astronauts, and presidents.
ISBN 0-689-82001-1
1. Rockwell, Norman, 1894-1978—Juvenile literature.
2. Painters—United States—Biography—Juvenile literature.
[1. Rockwell, Norman, 1894-1978. 2. Artists. 3. Art appreciation.] I. Title.
ND237.R68G45 1999
759.13—dc21 [B] 98-36546

CONTENTS

CHAPTER 1

Talent "Like a Bag of Lemon Drops"

NORMAN ROCKWELL WAS BORN IN 1894 in the family's "shabby brownstone" in New York City. Long before he became a household name, Norman Perceval Rockwell was a pale, skinny eight-year-old. The kids called him "Mooney" because of his thick glasses. They made fun of his black wool coat—a hand-me-down from his grandfather. They laughed at his awkward gait. His older brother, Jarvis, was a natural athlete, and that made Norman even more self-conscious about his clumsiness. There was not much he could do about that, but as quickly as he could, he burned the heavy coat with its black velvet lapels, and he dropped the middle name of Perceval, even though his mother told him it had belonged to an English hero.

Somehow he was able to forget about all of his physical deficiencies each night when his father picked up a novel by Charles Dickens and began to read. His father's voice may have been monotonous, but it didn't prevent Norman's imagination from soaring. He began sketching the characters: from *The Old Curiosity Shop*, the villain Quilp, young Kit, and Little Nell; and from *Oliver Twist*, Fagin and Sikes, the Artful Dodger, and Oliver himself. Jarvis sat at the table doing his homework. His mother sat near the gas lamp doing her mending while she listened.

Norman's pencil sketches were quick and imaginative. He brought the villains to life and made the young boys seem earnest and needy. He

Triple Self-Portrait. Saturday Evening Post cover, February 13, 1960.

had all the characters racing around the page. He also learned how complicated Dickens's characters were. Mr. Dick of *David Copperfield* was a "simpleton," but he was also "kindly, generous, loving" and filled with good common sense.

Norman's brother, Jarvis, could run and catch effortlessly. Norman discovered he could draw just as effortlessly. By age twelve he knew that that was what he wanted to do with his life. He felt everybody had something they could do. "Jarvis could jump over three orange crates; Jack Outwater had an uncle who had seen a pirate; George Dugan could wiggle his ears; I could draw," he said, in a matter-of-fact manner. "[My] ability was just something I had, like a bag of lemon drops."

With chalk he drew pictures on the sidewalk at the urging of his friends. He also made ships by drawing on pieces of cardboard and cutting them out so that Jarvis and his friends could carry on naval wars.

But deep down he still envied the other boys' physical grace and decided to do something about his puny body. Every morning he got up early to exercise. He did push-ups, jumping jacks, and knee bends. He was determined to get stronger and build up his muscles.

After a whole month of exercising, Norman looked in the mirror and discovered he looked exactly the same. He still had a long skinny neck and a bulging Adam's apple. He still had thin shoulders, "jelly" arms, and "measly-looking" legs. The exercises had not made a bit of difference, so he gave them up.

Every summer his father took the family to stay on a farm in upstate New York near the Catskills. There he and Jarvis swam in ponds, fished in lakes, searched for bullfrogs, and went on hayrides. They also helped with milking and picking crops. For Norman the chores never seemed like hard work because he was so happy to be in the country.

He captured that sense of joy in his painting *No Swimming*. Three boys and their dog are racing for their lives in front of a NO SWIMMING sign. The dog's fur is flying; so are their clothes. Although they are worried about getting caught, the boys are also exuberant as they race through the country setting.

Norman and Jarvis

The Champ. Saturday Evening Post cover, April 29, 1922.

Norman and a friend holding frogs

The Rockwell family

On the train ride home at the end of summer, Norman carried turtles and frogs to the city, but no matter how well he cared for them, they didn't thrive away from their natural surroundings and usually died after a few months.

Norman felt those summers influenced his later work because he gained a sense of freedom and an appreciation of the natural world while he lived in the country. He soon learned that cities could be dangerous places. Norman was only seven when President William McKinley was assassinated in front of a large crowd in Buffalo, New York.

By the eighth grade Norman was drawing all the time. Miss Julia Smith, his teacher, recognized how talented he was. She told him to draw pictures to go with his reports: "Revolutionary soldiers and covered wagons for history; birds, lions, fish, elephants for science." She urged him to draw a special Christmas picture on the blackboard.

Norman's mother didn't encourage him to become an artist, even though his maternal grandfather had been a portrait painter and his father was able to draw well enough to copy illustrations in magazines. Draw for a hobby, but find a respectable way to earn a living, she counseled.

Despite his mother's pleas, Norman knew he could not ignore his talent. Shocking everyone, he quit high school after his sophomore year, when he was only fifteen. He couldn't wait to begin art school. There he hoped to study every aspect of drawing and to learn all the technical aspects he would need to become a successful illustrator. Later in life he called his lack of higher education "a badge of honor" because he had accomplished so much without it.

No Swimming. Saturday Evening Post cover, June 4, 1921.

CHAPTER 2

"Live in the Picture"

Portrait of Norman at Art
Students League

NORMAN WAS BORN WITH A NATURAL ARTISTIC ABILITY, but to become
a fine illustrator, he knew he had to take his classes at art school seriously,
and he had to earn enough money to pay for them. By then his family had
left New York City and was living in the town of Mamaroneck, where
Norman found lawns to mow, leaves to rake, and art classes to teach.

He commuted to the National Academy of Design in the city,
where students drew from plaster casts of Mercury, Hercules, and Venus.
The casts were old and chipped. They were missing noses or fingers. But
they didn't move, and he could draw them endlessly. Norman studied
the curve of the head on those casts. He looked at the way the ear, if
there was an ear, attached to the head; the location of the nose, eyes,
and mouth in relation to one another. He looked at the way the back of
the head curved. He realized it was necessary to think of the whole head
even when he was sketching only the front of it.

He moved down the body, noting where the legs joined the torso.
He made many charcoal drawings of what he saw, always trying to
improve his accuracy.

Norman kept hearing about the Art Students League, which was
said to offer a warm atmosphere for young students. Before long he
signed up to take a drawing class at the league.

Every afternoon thirty-five men squeezed into a small space, set
out their large pads of drawing paper on easels, prepared their charcoal,
and waited for the model to undress behind a screen in the corner of the
room. League rules did not allow men and women to study a nude model
in the same classroom.

The men sketched for twenty-five minutes, light pouring in from enormous skylights above them. Then the model took a five-minute rest. One woman model might put on a kimono and stay behind the screen. A male model might sit on the platform to have a smoke. Another woman, comfortable without clothes, might pass from easel to easel, looking at the students' drawings.

George Bridgman, the teacher, moved around the room with a thick piece of charcoal, correcting students' work by drawing bold lines on their sketches. He showed one man how to shape the shoulder as it joined the neck, another how to turn the arm or the leg properly.

Mr. Bridgman was not encouraging. "Maybe two of you will make a success," he told the class. Each man dreamed that he would be one of the two. Norman was no different. But he wasn't going to depend on luck. He intended to work hard and make it happen. The other students called him "the Deacon" because he was so serious when he worked and wouldn't let anything interfere with his concentration.

He became class monitor, which saved him tuition fees. One of his duties was to select and pose the model and to announce the model's rest period. Another was to put away the skeleton after Mr. Bridgman had used it in class to explain the complex structure of the body and how interdependent all of the parts were. You couldn't draw a hand properly unless you knew what was underneath the skin. Mr. Bridgman told them that it took eleven muscles just to move a little finger.

Norman had grown up hearing about the "Golden Age" of illustration and seeing the work of fine illustrators like Howard Pyle, Winslow Homer, and N. C. Wyeth. He had seen the books they illustrated and knew their magazine covers.

In those days famous illustrators were treated with as much respect as portrait or landscape painters. Mr. Bridgman didn't distinguish

Bridgman's life class

between the type of artist either. He expected the same effort from all his students, no matter how they intended to use their artistic skills. Norman wanted to become an illustrator because he found it a "profession with a great tradition, a profession I could be proud of." He saw a fine illustrator as a recorder of both past and present, who insisted on accuracy in his work. If he was drawing a castle in Scotland or a Spanish ship, he needed to know how that castle or that ship really looked.

At the Art Students League, he also took Thomas Fogarty's illustration class. Mr. Fogarty was an excellent teacher who gave the students—men and women—practical assignments. He selected a story from a magazine, then asked the students to read it, to find a scene to illustrate, and to use authentic clothes and settings. He expected the students to know the characters and to "live in the picture." From him, Norman learned how crucial facial expressions are in an illustration.

Mr. Fogarty kept telling the students, "Painting a picture's like throwing a ball against a wall. Throw it hard, ball comes back hard. Feel a picture hard, public feels it the same way." He reminded them: "An illustration is an author's words in paint."

Norman won a scholarship at the end of his first year in Fogarty's class, and his picture of a small boy with mumps longingly watching the Fourth of July fireworks from his bedroom window was judged the best illustration for the year. The wistful child and his dog would be a recurring theme in his future work, as can be seen in the painting *Crackers in Bed.*

Crackers in Bed. Original oil for advertisement, Edison Mazda Lamp Works, 1920.

CHAPTER 3

An "Author's Words in Paint"

THREE YEARS PASSED WHILE NORMAN STUDIED ART. By then it was 1912, and he was almost eighteen. Mr. Fogarty believed he was ready to go out into the world for real illustrating jobs, not just classroom projects. He sent Norman to the Catholic Paulist Fathers, who were looking for an artist to illustrate their Christmas booklet. He cautioned Norman not to mention that he wasn't Catholic. But Norman proved to his teacher and the Fathers that he didn't have to be Catholic to draw wonderful children, angels, and a jolly Santa Claus for their holiday book.

After that Fogarty recommended him to a publishing house, where he was assigned to illustrate a children's book, *Tell Me Why Stories.* He was paid $150 to do ten or twelve illustrations, and it made him feel that he was on his way toward a successful career.

Before long the editor of *Boys' Life,* a Boy Scout magazine, asked him to illustrate a handbook on camping, and then he began to illustrate stories for the magazine. Soon he was asked to become the magazine's art director at a monthly salary of $50. Every month he painted the cover and illustrated one story.

He also illustrated for *St. Nicholas* magazine, which included stories by famous writers and by children who wrote poems and stories of their own.

Norman's reputation was growing. He was asked to illustrate books by authors who saw his work in magazines. Most of the pieces he did were of children in black and white or sepia and white, always using neighborhood boys and girls as his models.

About that time he and his parents moved to New Rochelle, which meant he had to find a whole new group of children to model for him. He stood near school yards and vacant lots where kids were playing, and when he found an expressive child, he offered the boy or girl fifty cents an hour to model for him.

The children were usually eager to earn the money, but they found posing much more difficult than they had expected. After only a few minutes, they were ready to quit. Something always started itching or made them sneeze.

Norman found a way to keep them still. He put a stack of nickels on the table. After the child had posed for twenty-five minutes, he put five nickels in a new stack to show the child what he or she had earned. That seemed to help. So did a stern look from a parent or an older sibling who came along to chaperone the model.

After a time Norman wanted a new challenge. His friend Clyde Forsythe, a cartoonist, who always gave him honest criticism, urged him to take his work around to adult magazines and book publishers.

Norman longed to draw a cover for the *Saturday Evening Post*. "In those days the cover of the *Post* was . . . the greatest show window in America for an illustrator. If you did a cover for the *Post* you had arrived." He sat in his studio looking at the magazine and fantasizing that it was his cover, that he had become famous doing *Post* covers. But he couldn't really imagine himself going to the magazine and facing the editor, George Horace Lorimer, who would probably laugh at him.

He mooned over it a lot until Clyde insisted he was good enough. "For Lord's sake, stop chewing on your tongue and do a cover."

All right, he would take Clyde's advice. He created a cover with a handsome man dressed in evening clothes, leaning over to kiss a beautiful woman—the type of cover he thought Mr. Lorimer would like. He did a second painting of a ballerina dancing onstage.

He showed the paintings to Clyde. Those are terrible, his friend said. Your woman looks like a "tomboy who's been scrubbed with a rough washcloth." And he picked up one of the *Boys' Life* covers. "Do

Norman with Wooden Case. Illustration from *My Adventures as an Illustrator,* 1960.

that," he said, pointing at it. "Do what you're best at. Kids."

Norman knew Clyde was right. He put away the early paintings, called his favorite model, Billy Paine, and went back to work. Billy had a wonderfully expressive face. Norman used his face for all three boys in the new picture he was painting. He completed two other paintings and made some sketches for possible covers. Then he had a wooden case built to carry his work. He bought a train ticket for Philadelphia and nervously left New York City. Once he arrived at the *Post* offices, he handed his paintings to a secretary, who asked him to wait while the art editor studied them. Nervously he sat with the large case on his lap, while staff members kept walking back and forth, wondering what Norman had concealed inside the enormous box. Finally one man stopped in front of him and pointed to the case. "Is the body in there now?" he asked, pretending that Norman was lugging a coffin around.

Growing more uneasy by the minute, Norman tried to ignore their stares and comments. At last, Walter Dower, the art editor, returned. He told Norman that both he and Mr. Lorimer liked his work. They wanted to buy the two paintings he had brought, as well as a sketch idea. But that wasn't all. They wanted Norman to do three additional covers for the magazine. And they would pay him! Seventy-five dollars for each cover.

He left the offices feeling like he was walking on air. He couldn't wait to get home to tell his family and to call his girlfriend, Irene O'Connor. After he told her his happy news, he asked her to marry him.

Joe with Dog Finds Man in Snow.
Boys' Life illustration, 1913.

CHAPTER 4

"The Greatest Show Window in America"

NORMAN'S FIRST SATURDAY EVENING POST COVER appeared on May 20, 1916. Called *Salutation* or *Boy with Baby Carriage*, it shows a young man, dressed in suit and tie, with a baby bottle in his breast pocket. He looks mortified when two friends see him pushing his baby sister in a pram. They are on their way to play baseball. One of them mockingly doffs his cap; the other is stifling a laugh. Billy Paine was the model for all three boys, but Norman changed his hair color, his facial expression, and even his teeth. Early covers used black, white, and red only, but Norman made the most of that limited palette.

Other magazine editors saw Norman's *Post* covers and asked him to do covers for them. And he began to receive fan mail telling him how much people loved his work and urging him to keep those covers coming.

When the United States declared war against Germany in 1917, Norman was determined to join the Navy. He rushed down to the recruiting office to sign up. The Navy sent him to Charleston, South Carolina, where the captain assigned him to the staff of the base newspaper. He didn't look sturdy enough to join the military action in Europe. Also, they quickly recognized Norman's artistic ability and put him to work drawing portraits of the men to send home to their wives or girlfriends.

Norman was also able to continue drawing *Post* covers as long as they related to the service. One cover showed two sailors comparing their messages from home. Another depicted a "doughboy" surrounded by marching kids.

Salutation (Boy with Baby Carriage). Rockwell's first Saturday Evening Post cover, May 20, 1916.

Norman was discharged in November 1918, after serving for almost a year. World War I was over, and he returned to Irene and his studio in New Rochelle. He continued to do *Post* covers and to illustrate advertising copy for products such as Jell-O and Fisk bicycle tires.

The *Saturday Evening Post* printed thousands of extra copies of the magazine when Norman's covers appeared because the public loved them. Many people remember waiting eagerly for the weekly magazine to arrive to discover if it had a Rockwell cover. If so, they carefully tore it from the rest of the magazine and pinned it to the wall. It touched their emotions and reminded them of youth, home, and the good life they were living.

Norman continued to do covers for the magazine for the next fifty-five years, averaging seven a year. There were a total of 332 covers, all of them telling an emotional and universal story about the way Americans lived. His great talent was that his paintings told stories without using a single word.

The *Post* included stories in serial form—perhaps a mystery by Agatha Christie or Sir Arthur Conan Doyle, or a novelette or romance. There were articles about people on Wall Street, the discovery of penicillin, the men who served in the government, and the labor movement.

In 1927, when Charles Lindbergh became a national hero after his solo flight across the Atlantic Ocean, Norman decided to paint the handsome young pilot as a pioneer of the skies, just as the early explorers and pilgrims had been pioneers on the ground. But this was a rush job. He had only one day in which to complete the painting and get it to the magazine before it became old news. Quickly he found a model and an aviator's cap and worked around the clock for twenty-six hours.

The *Saturday Evening Post* was read in millions of American homes. The editors made sure that the magazine's covers were not controversial or upsetting. They wanted the art to be in good taste and to not offend a single reader. Norman thought up several ideas and did rough sketches. He went into the office to show them to the art editor. Then he acted them out, showing what each character would do. After

Pioneer of the Air.
Saturday Evening Post cover, July 23, 1927.

Norman and Mary

Norman and Mary's three sons:
Thomas, Jarvis, and Peter

the editor approved his ideas, Norman went home to paint the actual covers.

While Norman and Irene were married, they led a very social life. They went boating and played bridge and golf. They went to parties and gave them at home and at the country club. But Norman was happiest working, not playing, and he realized the marriage was not a good one for either of them. He and Irene divorced in 1929.

The following year, when he went to visit friends in California, he met Mary Barstow, a schoolteacher. They fell in love, married that April, and moved back to New Rochelle. Their first son, Jarvis, was born in 1931. Thomas was born in 1933, and Peter in 1936.

Mary read aloud to Norman while he painted. Sometimes she read Dickens. Other times she read Jane Austen's novels, or Leo Tolstoy's *War and Peace,* or selections from *The Harvard Classics,* which he'd purchased to complete his education. Sometimes he listened to opera or to a Yankees baseball game on the radio.

By 1939 the family had moved to Arlington, Vermont, to live near friends who were also illustrators. The whole town soon became involved in modeling for Norman or in helping him find props, make props, or get anything else he needed. When he got stuck in the middle of a painting, he asked Mary or their sons or their neighbors for advice. Usually he ended up doing exactly what he had wanted to do in the first place.

Every week he and Mary went square dancing at the West Arlington Grange Hall, just across the road from their house. Norman built a studio out of a converted barn in front of the house, and the boys were in and out of the studio, offering their opinions, sometimes posing for Norman, sometimes trying to get him to come out and play ball with them. Often it was boring for them to stand around watching him paint. "He worked slowly, with great detail, and you hardly saw anything change," Thomas said. If only he had been an artist like Jackson Pollock with his "splashing and splattering of paint." Then it would have been perfect for kids to watch.

Norman's studio burned down in the summer of 1943, just a few

nights after he had completed four major works and taken them to the
Post. Thomas was the first to notice flames shooting from the studio. He
alerted Norman, who rushed outside but couldn't get near the building
to save a thing. Mary bundled Thomas and his brothers in blankets so
they could watch through the window. All three of them
had measles. Neighbors rushed over to help. Volunteer
firemen arrived, but none of them were able to save the
studio.

They just sat on the lawn watching the building
burn. Norman had lost everything. Gone were his original artworks, including many *Post* covers; all his brushes
and paints; other artists' work; all his costumes and
props; and the sketches he had been working on of
President Franklin Roosevelt and the White House.

As sad as he felt, Norman was still able to make a
humorous vignette of drawings called *My Studio Burns,*
showing the events of that July night.

Later he and Mary decided to move closer to
West Arlington. They bought a house on the village
green near the one-room schoolhouse and the
Grange. He had a new studio built right behind the
house, but it would never be the same. He could
replace his easel and paints and other art supplies, but
he would never be able to replace the costumes and
props he had used for his early historical scenes. As a
result, his future covers would be more concerned
with the present than the past. Fortunately it was a time when editors
were not as interested in using historical pictures as they had been
earlier.

In those years Norman did a great many magazine illustrations
that were easy for him because he could "romp right through them,"
while with *Post* covers he had to come up with an idea and then figure
out the best way to show it. Even though covers were the hardest for
him, they were always his favorite work.

My Studio Burns. Illustration, *Saturday
Evening Post* story, July 17, 1943.

CHAPTER 5

Lost in Tom Sawyer's Cave

Schoolmaster Flogging Tom Sawyer.
Illustration, *Adventures of Tom Sawyer*, 1936.

Tom and Becky in the Cave. Illustration,
Adventures of Tom Sawyer, 1936.

THE FIRST THING NORMAN DID when he was asked to illustrate Mark Twain's *Tom Sawyer* and *Huckleberry Finn* was to reread both books, searching for powerful scenes to illustrate.

Next he traveled to Hannibal, Missouri, Twain's hometown. There he discovered that Twain's descriptions on the pages of the books were not fictionalized. They actually existed. He found Aunt Polly's house with the drainpipe that Twain had climbed down as a boy and saw the spot where he landed on the woodpile. He paced the steps to Becky Thatcher's house. Just as Norman suspected, Tom Sawyer's haunts in the book had been Mark Twain's actual boyhood settings.

He asked a local man to lead him to the cave Becky and Tom had explored. The man guided him there and said he would return later to escort Norman back to his hotel; he couldn't stay because his wife was afraid to be home alone. There was talk of escaped bank robbers in Hannibal.

Norman carried his acetylene lamp and wound his way down into the cave, all the time remembering what Mark Twain had written in *Tom Sawyer*:

> In one place [Becky and Tom] found a spacious cavern from whose ceiling depended a multitude of shining stalactites of the length and circumference of a man's leg; . . . Under the roof, vast knots of bats had packed themselves together, thousands in a bunch; the lights disturbed the creatures and they came flocking down by hundreds, squeaking and darting furiously at the candles . . . a bat struck Becky's light out with its wing while she was passing out of the cavern.

Norman made sketches of the rocks within the cave, showing how they were piled one on top of another in some places. And before he knew it, his own lantern blew out. He was left in total darkness. The smooth rock he sat on turned into a block of ice. The air around him grew colder. He listened. There was not a single sound.

Norman tried to stay calm. He knew the man would be back for him soon, and he had made some good sketches before his lamp blew out. But it was so dark in the cave. And suddenly the silence changed. He heard sounds overhead. More bats perhaps. Then scrabblings below. Mice? Now he knew how terrified Becky and Tom were when they were lost in this same cave.

After what seemed like hours, he spotted a tiny light in the distance. Was it his guide returning? Or was it the escaped criminals? Closer and closer the light came, growing brighter with every step. His skin prickled. His heart hammered. He thought to hide. But before he could move, the light was upon him, filling the small space.

It was his guide! With great relief, he followed the man through the cave to the entrance and the evening's dusk.

The next day Norman continued to explore the town. He waited on Main Street and offered to buy worn clothes from those folks who passed him. He paid a farmer five dollars for his tattered pants, another for his overalls. He bought straw hats, sunbonnets, and gingham dresses. Even a horse's hat. He wanted to return to his studio with authentic clothing for his models to wear when he made his drawings. It wouldn't do to find new clothes and make them appear old. He needed clothes that had been worn for years and looked it.

Another important goal was to make Tom, Becky, and the other children in the books look like real children, not like short adults. Often artists in the past had drawn young people just as they drew adults, with grown-up facial expressions and postures. Norman captured the inner emotions of his child models as well as their physical qualities.

As he had learned in art school, it was absolutely necessary for an illustrator to know the actual scene he was drawing and to use the correct clothing and props. Shortly after he completed the Twain illustrations, he went to Concord, Massachusetts, to see Louisa May Alcott's home for an article about the author of *Little Women* he was to illustrate. Norman spent hours in her home, sketching the attic where she had written, her bedroom, her rocker, the lace curtains and the hooked rugs.

All three projects were well received, and Norman felt it was because he had been in the settings and seen the small details, rather than trying to make them up.

Louisa May Alcott in Her Attic at Concord, Massachusetts. Illustration, *Women's Home Companion*, 1937.

CHAPTER 6

"Kid with the Camera Eye"

ALTHOUGH BOOKS, CALENDARS, and advertisements were an important part of Norman's work, the *Saturday Evening Post* covers were his mainstay. They were "the first thing he thought about in the morning, and the last thing he thought about at night," one biographer said. He lived with the pressure of deadlines, as an early cover painting shows.

He needed an idea before he could begin sketching. Sometimes the idea came easily. Sometimes it didn't. Waiting for an idea to hatch, he sat doodling at the easel, got up and walked around, sat back down at the easel, and made a few more attempts. Sometimes he drew a sailor leaning on a lamppost, hoping that would get him started.

But it was when he least expected it, just waking up in the morning or while shaving, that an idea would come to him, "lighting up the inside of [his] head like a flash of lightning in a dark sky."

Once he had the idea, the next challenge was to find the perfect model to tell his story. Early in his career he worked only with live models. He rushed to capture their poses before they took a rest or before the light changed in the room.

He sat for hours, yelling, "Up eyebrows!" "Raise that arm a little!" and "Make the smile bigger!" He demonstrated every gesture and every facial expression, and by the end of the day he was exhausted. Other illustrators began using photographers to capture their scenes, but Norman and his friends refused. Norman felt so strongly about this, he had even called it cheating or plagiarism to draw from photographs.

But by the mid-1930s, he noticed that his covers were all done

Deadline. Saturday Evening Post cover, October 8, 1938.

from the same angles because he always drew from his easel. Maybe he should try photography after all. He set up the scene for his model, arranged the props, and hired a photographer to take hundreds of shots. He discovered that it made a tremendous difference. Photographs provided him many more angles and details all at once, and he didn't have to keep a model for days when that person needed to be back on the farm or in the classroom.

Once the photographs were developed, he spread them out all over the floor and chose the ones he liked best. Then he made a few small pencil sketches to organize his material. At last he was ready to do a full-size charcoal drawing. He liked to vary the size from time to time, but he never did a cover so large that it wouldn't fit in a taxicab or a car for its trip to the *Post*'s office in Philadelphia. Sometimes he made the painting as small as the actual cover would be (eleven-by-eleven inches) but most of the time he painted large oils and let the art director reduce them to fit the magazine.

He transferred the charcoal layout to a canvas, either by tracing it with special tracing paper or by using a projector called a balopticon to enlarge the image onto a canvas that might be four feet tall.

At last he was ready to start working in color. He was always nervous that he would get tense and spoil the painting, but it rarely happened. The final painting could take a few days or a few weeks, depending upon how complicated the picture was.

Once the work was completed, he framed it to present it to the art director. Without the frame, the editor might look at the rough, unfinished edges of the canvas and not get the full impact of the painting. Norman once said, "The poorer the picture, the better the frame." Plus, it protected the painting when it was lugged from Vermont to Pennsylvania.

When he was beginning his career, people always called him "the kid with the camera eye" because he captured a scene so accurately. Now he added the actual camera lens to his own good eye, and the combination made his work richer and even more interesting.

Norman using a balopticon to enlarge his drawing

CHAPTER 7

"Average People Doing Average Things"

NORMAN WAS FORTY-SEVEN WHEN WORLD WAR II BEGAN—too old to serve. But it was in his thoughts, in everyone's thoughts, because young men were being drafted, food items were being rationed, newspapers and rubber products were being recycled for the war effort, and there were frequent air-raid drills. He wanted to reflect the mood around him, but he did not want to draw covers concentrating on battle scenes.

He decided there was another way. He could tell the story of the war through the experiences of a fictional young man who had just enlisted in the Army. One night at the Grange square dance, he noticed Bob Buck, the perfect person to be his model. Mary nicknamed him "Willie Gillis" because she had been reading "Wee Willie Winkie" to the boys.

Norman painted scenes of Bob at the USO, reading the hometown newspaper when he should have been peeling apples on KP duty, sitting solemnly in church, and getting food packages from home.

In a later cover, Norman painted portraits on the wall of six generations of Gillis men in their uniforms, from the time of the Revolutionary War right through to present-day Willie wearing his helmet. Below the portraits are books with such titles as *A History of the United States and the Gillis Family; The Gillis Family Genealogy;* and *Gillis at Gettysburg,* all made up by Norman. Thinking they were real titles, many people wrote to the magazine asking where they could buy the books.

The Gillis Heritage. Saturday Evening Post cover, September 16, 1944.

There were eleven Gillis covers in all, and by then Willie seemed like a real person to all the readers of the *Post.* They wanted to know what happened to him after the war, so Norman painted him as a college student using a grant under the GI Bill to pay for his education, as so many young men did.

Rosie the Riveter was another painting he made during the war to show life on the home front. Rosie represents the many women who went to work in factories to replace the men who had enlisted. She is dressed in overalls; her feet are stomping on Adolf Hitler's book, *Mein Kampf*; and her muscular arms and haughty expression tell the enemy to beware. In the background is a swirling American flag. Rosie is taking a lunch break, but not for long—the riveting tool rests on her lap.

In 1942, Norman had heard President Franklin Roosevelt give a speech explaining that the free world was fighting the war to protect every individual's right to freedom of speech and worship, as well as freedom from want and fear. But the president had used words that were so "darned high-blown," Norman couldn't figure out a way to show them.

One night when he was tossing and turning, he suddenly remembered how his neighbor had stood up at a town meeting to give his opinion. No one liked what he said, but they had listened to him. Well, that was freedom of speech, Norman realized. He could show that as one of the freedoms, then show the other three freedoms in the same concrete way. They didn't have to be highfalutin' concepts.

He got so excited that he started to call his friend Mead Schaeffer, who was also an illustrator, and then realized it was 3:00 A.M. Instead, he got on his bike and rode over to Schaef's. It didn't seem to matter that he would wake him either way. He just had to share his ideas.

Norman made many sketches for each of the *Four Freedoms* illustrations and took them to Washington, D.C., trying to convince government agencies to sponsor his paintings for the war effort. No one was interested, and at first Norman felt very discouraged. Then he decided to take his sketches to Ben Hibbs, who was then *Post* editor. He loved Norman's sketches and told him to forget about doing covers or advertisements for the time being. Just concentrate on the *Four Freedoms.*

Rosie the Riveter. Saturday Evening Post cover, May 29, 1943.

Norman thought it would be easy. He began with *Freedom of Speech* and drew his neighbor standing up at the town meeting to speak his piece. But the first attempts didn't work. He had too many people in the scene. You couldn't tell what the man was doing. He tried again and again, until he finally realized the only way to capture the power of the moment was to have one man become the focus of the painting.

There he is. Standing tall, with the town's annual report in his jacket pocket, an earnest look on his face, a sense of silence in the room as his neighbors listen intently to his words. There may be a whole roomful of neighbors, but Norman shows only a few. Behind the speaker is a stark, empty blackboard, taking up almost half of the canvas and powerfully framing the man's figure.

Norman used himself in the painting, as he often did. It's difficult to spot him because there is only a tiny bit of his face, one ear cocked to hear the words, one eye attentive to the speaker.

For *Freedom of Worship*, he struggled again. Then he thought of the quote "Each according to the dictates of his own conscience," and he realized he could show a group of people worshiping by creating a montage of heads and praying hands. One woman is holding a rosary; a man wearing a Jewish yarmulke, or skullcap, on his head holds a small Bible. There is no background setting or story connected with the praying people, but it gives a powerful sense of respect for the differences in our society.

Four Freedoms signing, Hecht's Department Store, Washington, D.C., April 1943.

For *Freedom from Want*, Norman painted a family gathered around a Thanksgiving table. Grandmother brings a well-browned turkey; Grandfather has his carving tools handy. The colors of the scene are all subdued. Grandfather's dark suit pulls our eye into the painting, while the dishes and tablecloth are white. The bowl of fruit on the table blends in with the brown tones of the family's hair. Their smiling faces form a border around the painting, some of them looking toward the viewer.

In *Freedom from Fear*, two parents are checking on their sleeping children in what appears to be a quiet, peaceful scene. Only the newspaper in the father's hand gives us a clue to the larger story. An upside-down headline, partially visible, reads: BOMBING KI . . . Beneath that headline is another barely readable heading: WOMEN AND CHILDREN SLAUGHTERED BY RAIDS. Now the point is made.

London was constantly being bombed by the Germans during World War II, and English parents could never put their children to bed without fear. Instead of painting a scene of devastation and death, Norman chose to interpret President Roosevelt's "freedom from fear" by showing that all parents wish they could keep their children safe from outside danger.

It took him more than six months to complete these four large paintings. The *Post* used them inside the magazine, each painting next to an essay about the subject, and they were so successful that the government at last decided to use the paintings for a campaign to sell war bonds. Norman toured with the paintings, and nearly $133 million in war bonds were sold. He felt he had made a positive contribution to the war effort.

Ben Hibbs hung *Freedom of Worship* and *Freedom of Speech* in his office at the *Post* after the tour and insisted they were "great human documents in the form of paint and canvas."

Norman was more down-to-earth in the way he defined the *Four Freedoms* series. He thought the paintings "showed average people doing average things," and that was how he could "portray the loftiest ideas."

Clockwise from upper left:
Freedom of Speech
Freedom of Worship
Freedom from Fear
Freedom from Want

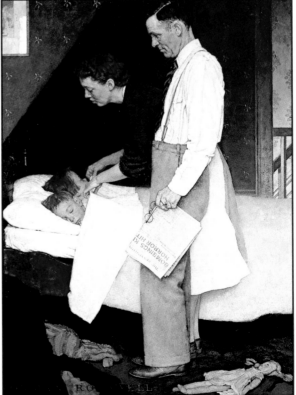

CHAPTER 8

From Tears to Laughter

IN 1953, NORMAN AND MARY MOVED to Stockbridge, Massachusetts. Mary was not well, and she had been regularly seeing physicians there. When the harsh winter months came, it was too difficult for her to continue commuting from Vermont.

They found a comfortable house, and it did not take long for them to fit into their new community. Norman continued to paint *Post* covers as he had always done, and he quickly began a search for new models in the Stockbridge area. He was said to be a genius at knowing which children to choose.

Norman's sons were growing up and so were his models. The painting *Breaking Home Ties,* from 1954, reflects this change.

Here a father and son are sitting on the running board of an old truck. The young man, dressed in a suit and bold tie, sits up straight, watching for the train that is going to take him to college. At his feet is a suitcase with a STATE U pennant and a stack of books, already marked by bookmarks.

His weary dad, back bent in resignation, holds his weather-beaten hat and his son's new hat. He won't look in the direction of the train—it's coming to take his son away. Just as mournful is the dog, his snout resting on the young man's leg.

For Norman the painting reflected a painful change in his own life because Jarvis, his oldest son, had just enlisted in the Air Force. Norman found it difficult to express the emotional scene. In the first versions he had a whole family sitting inside the train station. Then he moved outdoors and left the mother home, even though we assume that the neatly wrapped package with a pink bow the young man holds contains sandwiches she made for his trip.

Norman didn't have daughters, but he understood a girl's longing to grow up. That same year he painted *Girl at the Mirror,* showing a pensive young girl sitting before a full-length mirror, her doll discarded on the floor. On her lap is a magazine featuring the movie star Jane Russell. She has pinned her braid up high and put on lipstick. *Will I ever grow up?* the girl seems to be asking. *Will I be beautiful when I do grow up?* His wife, Mary, said that it was one of Norman's favorite paintings.

Mary took care of everything so that Norman could work. She organized their finances and social life. She managed the house and meals, along with the boys' needs as they were growing up. And then suddenly, when she was fifty-one, she died in her sleep of a heart attack.

Now Norman was really alone. The boys were grown and away at school, in the service, and working. No longer would Mary be there to read Dickens or Jane Austen to him while he worked, or to encourage him to get on with a painting when he was caught up in the small details.

Work was such a habit for Norman that he tried to stick to his schedule of getting to the studio first thing in the morning and going back there after supper, but he missed Mary terribly. Sometimes he left the studio and walked around town looking lost, his pipe unlit, his mind somewhere else.

Before Mary died Norman had been working on a book about his life. At first he tried using a Dictaphone, but he wasn't comfortable talking to himself. He felt too self-conscious. His son Thomas agreed to let "Pop" tell him stories and to take notes. He found that Norman's stories improved each time he told them, and although perhaps the truth was stretched a bit, they both enjoyed putting the book together.

Norman dedicated *My Adventures as an Illustrator* to Mary and included a youthful sketch of her along with the words TO MARY, WHOSE LOVING HELP HAS MEANT SO MUCH TO ME.

Friends and family encouraged Norman to get out more, and so he signed up for a poetry class taught by a retired English teacher, Molly

Breaking Home Ties. Saturday Evening Post cover, September 25, 1954.

Girl at the Mirror. Saturday Evening Post cover, March 6, 1954.

Punderson. Norman liked studying the poetry, but when he didn't understand some of the lines in a Robert Frost poem, he suggested calling Frost to ask what the poet had meant, instead of sitting around in the classroom trying to come up with an answer off the top of their heads.

With that attitude, Norman stood out in the class. He found the teacher interesting, and she was intrigued by her student. Before long, Norman and Molly decided to marry. After their October 1961 marriage, they traveled together around the world.

Norman had produced Christmas covers for the *Post* almost every year since 1919. Some show characters straight out of a Dickens novel, including the famous painting of Tiny Tim from *A Christmas Carol* blessing everyone, painted in 1934. Others show a jovial Santa making out gift lists for children, dozing while his elves work, or studying the globe as he plans his trip to every home.

One of Norman's favorite young models was Scott Ingram, who posed for the *Post* Christmas cover, titled *Discovery* in 1956, showing a small boy who is shocked when he discovers Santa's suit in his dad's bureau drawer. About a month before Christmas, Norman dropped by the Ingram home with a pair of pajamas several sizes too big for Scotty. "Scotty, you wear those pajamas tonight, tomorrow, and the next night, all right?" Norman said.

Then he turned to Scotty's mother with the warning, "Don't wash them!"

Four days later Scotty took his wrinkled pajamas and went to Norman's studio, where all the props had been assembled. Norman told Scotty to put on his pajamas and stand in front of the bureau, looking as surprised as he could. But that didn't quite do it.

"Make believe that you just saw a ghost," Norman suggested. And now Scotty's shocked look was perfect. There he stands, wearing

Norman and Molly

enormous flannel pajamas, eyes wide with amazement, and Santa's beard in his hand.

Apparently many parents were upset by the cover and sent angry letters to the magazine because they didn't want their children to question the existence of Santa Claus. For once Norman's idea had backfired.

That was not the case with the three April Fool's Day covers he painted in which he purposely drew everything upside down and backward. He showed a man fishing in the middle of winter, or a couple playing a game indoors while geese fly through the scene, a skunk sits on the woman's lap, a deer rests underneath the man's chair, and mushrooms grow out of the carpet.

One year he painted the inside of an antique shop with the owner and his young customer set into a topsy-turvy world. The shopkeeper's head is on all the dolls. A cat has the head of a dog and the tail of a raccoon. Ivy is growing around a hot potbellied stove. The skunk and deer are here again. It is one of his most surreal paintings.

Norman thought he knew how many deliberate mistakes he made in each of these covers, but his viewers always found many more.

His holiday covers convey a wonderful sense of whimsy. So do his self-portraits. You have to search for him in *Freedom of Speech*. He's even harder to recognize when he's wearing a wig or dressed as a minister. His pipe is almost always in his hand or his mouth, or even in his back pocket—a lucky talisman for him whether he was smoking it or not.

The model for the April Fool painting

The Discovery. Saturday Evening Post Christmas cover, 1956.

April Fool: Girl with Shopkeeper. Saturday Evening Post cover, April 3, 1948.

CHAPTER 9

Splash, Drip, and Spatter

ONE OF NORMAN'S FAVORITE PAINTERS was Pablo Picasso. He studied Picasso's work and the way he had influenced artists around the world to experiment with new methods. He saw how one American artist, Jackson Pollock, developed new art forms by spattering and dripping paint on huge canvases to create thick textures and interesting shapes.

Norman kept wondering if he should stop telling stories about people's lives and try to paint in a new way. In the painting called *Connoisseur*, done for a *Post* cover in 1962, he decided to experiment. He would make his own "Jackson Pollock." He took off his shoes, mixed paint in paper cups, and put canvases on the floor. He splashed paint, he dripped paint, he spattered paint. He made patterns all over the canvas and paper. The floor was covered. So was he, but now he had a background for a modern painting.

He set the abstract work into a frame on the wall of a museum and placed in front of it an elegant businessman wearing a pearl gray suit, holding a gray hat, matching kid gloves, and a long black umbrella behind his back. His shiny black shoes are planted on the floor in a dancer's second position. He is so close to the painting, his nose seems to be touching the art. Certainly not the best way to view a massive modern work. But even if he moved across the room, the man still might be puzzled by the painting.

There is no question Norman enjoyed making the abstract work. You can see that in the photograph of him splattering the paint. It's fun to play with paint; it makes an interesting work of art. *Or does it?* the businessman seems to be asking.

Rockwell at work painting the background for *Connoisseur*

Immediately after he painted *Connoisseur,* he went back to his usual covers for the *Post,* but things were changing at the magazine. Now they often asked Norman to paint portraits of famous politicians or government leaders. When he and Molly traveled around the world, he sketched world leaders—Jawaharlal Nehru in India and Gamal Abdel Nasser in Egypt—for use on future covers. At home he painted presidents and candidates: Dwight D. Eisenhower, Richard M. Nixon, John F. Kennedy.

Abraham Lincoln was a favorite subject for Norman. He painted him as a lawyer trying cases with iron determination and as a young man studying whenever he could. With an axe in one hand on his way to split logs and a book in the other, Norman portrays Lincoln as well as himself. Both of them used every minute to work. Both of them valued learning. And nothing was too hard for either of them, as is also evident in a photograph taken of Norman painting the young Lincoln. He had to climb up on three tall boxes to paint the very tall canvas.

Finally in 1963, Norman made a major decision to leave the *Post* after almost half a century of working for the magazine. It meant giving up the security of that long relationship, but he was ready for a change. In a sense, Norman was leaving the safety of his home in the same way his young man had in the painting *Breaking Home Ties.*

Norman painting Abraham Lincoln

Connoisseur. Saturday Evening Post cover, January 13, 1962.

CHAPTER 10

Controversy on Canvas

LOOK MAGAZINE IMMEDIATELY OFFERED NORMAN a new challenge. Go out into the world and show our readers what you find. He had always been concerned about social problems and yet had never been able to express that concern in his *Post* covers.

Norman said that he was "wildly excited about painting contemporary subjects . . . pictures about civil rights, astronauts, the Peace Corps, the poverty program. It's wonderful!"

In the 1964 painting *The Problem We All Live With*, Norman painted a scene showing Ruby Bridges, an eight-year-old black girl with pigtails, being escorted to a New Orleans school by four federal marshals, two in front and two behind her. The painting shows every detail of Ruby, from her white shoes and socks, to her notebook, ruler, and freshly ironed dress.

What it doesn't show are the faces of the marshals. The viewer sees their bodies

Norman painting *The Problem We All Live With*

dressed in suits with yellow armbands, and a letter in the pocket of one man, perhaps the actual integration order. But without their faces, the painting focuses on Ruby—her isolation, her vulnerability, the need for her to have such protection. The men's bodies stand like pillars around her, protecting her from the shouts and taunts of the unseen angry mob around the school.

In the background we see a smashed tomato someone has thrown against the wall and huge letters spelling out the epithets NIGGER and KKK.

Forty years later the painting still describes a scene of school integration better than many history books or newspaper columns could ever do and is a commentary on a painful moment in our country.

Norman also painted *New Kids in the Neighborhood,* showing a black family moving into a white neighborhood, but one gets the feeling the children will work it out without help from parents or other adults. They stand and look at one another with curiosity, but it shouldn't take long before the new boy is invited to bring his mitt and play baseball.

For years Norman rode his bicycle around Stockbridge every day, but he found he was "getting old" in his legs. He continued to travel and paint, and he even wrote and illustrated a children's book with Molly's help when he was in his late sixties. But he didn't have the same energy he had had in earlier years. "I work from fatigue to fatigue. At my age there's only so much daylight left," he admitted.

In May 1976, the town honored Norman with a huge parade down Main Street. There were floats representing his famous *Saturday Evening Post* covers, some with the actual models he'd used. There were marching bands and antique fire engines from the local communities.

When he was in his eighties he continued to go to his studio every day, sometimes in a wheelchair, but he rarely painted. Instead, he was cheered by visits from neighbors or friends. He died in November 1978 "of being eighty-four," Molly said. On his easel there was an unfinished canvas.

Thousands attended his funeral in Stockbridge. Boy Scouts and Cub Scouts lined the entrance to the church to honor the man who had painted their annual calendars for over fifty years.

During the service a poem was read about a man who loved his "fellowmen" above all. That was a fitting tribute for Norman Rockwell, who loved both young and old and was sensitive to their innermost feelings. He understood a parent's fears, a child's joy and longing, even a pet's loyalty. He "took his work seriously, but not himself."

As an illustrator, Norman Rockwell mirrored our emotions. He also painted our social history, beginning with idyllic country scenes, couples riding in horse and buggies, then carriages, and finally, Model-T Fords. He painted the latest inventions, from electricity to radio to television. There were scenes of war on the home front, portraits of world leaders and presidents of the United States. And in his later years he gave us pictures about the civil rights movement, school integration, and the Peace Corps.

By 1969, Norman came full circle when he painted an astronaut taking his first step on the moon. From Charles Lindbergh to Neil Armstrong, from the simple airplane *Spirit of St. Louis* to the complex lunar vehicle *Apollo 11,* Norman had observed enormous changes in his lifetime.

He explained that the illustrator "can show what has become so familiar that it is no longer noticed," and when we look back at the enormous legacy of his work, we are able to vividly relive those years and observe the enormous changes. The only thing that didn't change was Norman Rockwell. "He never lost his belief in the fundamental decency of his fellow human beings."

Art critics dismissed Norman's work. It wasn't real art, they said. It was corny, too sentimental. They didn't include it in serious studies of the art world, and sometimes that made Norman sad. But in a sense he has had broader influence. His work appears constantly, reflecting a moment from the past while defining a problem of today. Just recently, a Rockwell painting was found on the business pages of the *New York Times* accompanying an article about medical care. There is the kindly

The Problem We All Live With. Look illustration, January 14, 1964.

doctor, stethoscope in his ears, listening to a doll's heart while the worried young "mother" watches. Without a single word, the painting says we, too, want a caring physician to keep us well.

His work touches chords of emotional response, a reminder of an earlier time when life was simpler and better, as the past always seems to be—a time when we cared about our country, our family, and the neighbor down the street. That was what Norman Rockwell epitomized—that kind of caring. His paintings will continue to be meaningful even if the models do wear dated clothing and ride around in old-fashioned automobiles. Their emotions remain universal and timeless.

His paintings hang in the important museums of the country: the Metropolitan Museum of Art, the Brooklyn Museum, and the Corcoran Gallery, as well as the Norman Rockwell Museum in Stockbridge, Massachusetts. Thousands of people visit the Rockwell Museum every year because they value his paintings and the stories those paintings tell.

Important Dates

1894   Born in New York City

1909   Attends National Academy of Design

1910   Art Students League

1912   Illustrates *Tell Me Why Stories, St. Nicholas, American Boy, Boys' Life*

1916   First *Saturday Evening Post* cover

           Joins the Navy

           Marries Irene O'Connor (divorced after fourteen years)

1930   Marries Mary Barstow

1932   Studies in Paris

1935   Illustrates *Tom Sawyer* and *Huckleberry Finn*

1937   Illustrates Louisa May Alcott article

1939   Moves to Arlington, Vermont

1942   Paints *Four Freedoms* series

1953   Moves to Stockbridge, Massachusetts

1959   Mary dies

1961   Marries Molly Punderson

1963   Last *Post* cover

1964   *Look* magazine covers

1978   Dies at age eighty-four

1985   Molly dies

NOTES

COVER PHOTO: "Soda Jerk" was the nickname for a person who worked behind the counter of a soda fountain. Both soda fountains and soda jerks are now rare species.

CHAPTER 1

p. 1 "shabby brownstone" My *Adventures as an Illustrator as Told to Thomas Rockwell* (New York: Doubleday & Co., 1960), p. 29.

p. 2 "simpleton . . . loving" *Adventures*, p. 37.

"Jarvis . . . lemon drops." Ibid., p.47.

p. 4 "Revolutionary soldiers . . . science." Ibid., p. 56.

"badge of honor." Thomas Rockwell, telephone interview with author, October 9, 1997.

CHAPTER 2

p. 7 "Maybe . . . a success." *Adventures*, p. 76.

p. 9 "profession . . . proud of." Ibid., p. 70.

"live in . . . same way." Ibid., pp. 87, 88.

"An illustration . . . in paint." Donald Walton, *A Rockwell Portrait* (Kansas City, MO: Sheed Andrews & McMeel, Inc., 1978), p. 46.

CHAPTER 3

p. 11 In today's world an illustrator would not dare approach children directly. He would frighten them and appear suspicious to their parents and teachers.

"In those . . . arrived." *Adventures*, p. 130.

"For Lord's . . . cover." Ibid., p. 131.

"tomboy . . . Kids." Ibid., p. 131.

p. 12 "Is the . . . now?" Ibid., p. 133.

CHAPTER 4

p. 18 "He worked . . . paint." Thomas Rockwell, telephone interview.

p. 19 "romp right . . . them." *Adventures*, p. 302.

CHAPTER 5

p. 20 "In one . . . cavern." Mark Twain, *The Adventures of Tom Sawyer* (Norwalk, CT: The Easton Press, 1995), p. 247.

CHAPTER 6

p. 24 "the first . . . night." Karol Ann Marling, *Norman Rockwell* (New York: Harry N. Abrams, Inc., in association with the National Museum of American Art, Smithsonian Institution, 1997), p. 63.

"lighting up . . . sky." *Adventures*, p. 229.

"Up eyebrows! . . . bigger!" Rufus Jarman, "The Dickens of the Paintbrush," *New Yorker*, March 17, 1945, p. 37.

p. 26 "the poorer . . . frame." Arthur L. Guptill, *Norman Rockwell Illustrator* (New York: Ballantine Books, 1976) p. 208.

Man on the Moon. Look illustration, January 10, 1967.

CHAPTER 7

p. 28 USO, or United Service Organizations, provided food and social settings for our enlisted men during the war.

KP, or kitchen police, duty in the service referred to the kitchen work enlisted men performed as they assisted the cooks.

p. 30 The GI Bill paid for former servicemen to attend college after the war ended.
"darned high-blown." *Adventures,* p. 339.

p. 32 "great human . . . canvas." Ibid., p. 344.

p. 32 "showed average . . . ideas." *Norman Rockwell and the Saturday Evening Post,* produced and directed by Lewis Sayer Schwartz, 1986, videotape. Arlington Gallery, Arlington, VT.

CHAPTER 8

p. 38 "Scotty, you . . . them!" Scott Ingram, in Herschell Gordon Lewis, *Symbol of America: Norman Rockwell* (Huntington Valley, PA: Lynell Marketing, Inc., 1982), p. 126.

"Make believe . . . ghost." Ibid., p. 128.

CHAPTER 10

p. 46 "wildly excited . . . wonderful!" quote on wall of Norman Rockwell Museum, originating from a speech given by Rockwell.

In May 1954, the United States Supreme Court outlawed racial segregation in public schools in the case of *Brown versus the Board of Education.* Separate schools for blacks and whites would no longer be constitutional. But that didn't mean schools immediately changed. In Norman's painting, one black child is being escorted to school by federal marshals in a New Orleans school as late as 1960.

p. 47 "I work . . . left." Marling, *Norman Rockwell,* p. 149.

"of being eighty-four." Deanne Durrett, *The Importance of Norman Rockwell* (San Diego: Lucent Books, Inc., 1997), p. 82.

p. 50 As recalled by Ingram, in Lewis, *Symbol of America,* p. 239. The poem read, "Abou Ben Adhem"—one of Rockwell's favorites—includes the lines: "I pray thee, then / Write me as one that loves his fellowmen."

"took his . . . himself." Don Spalding, phone interview with Susan Meyer on audiotape, October 7, 1980.

Before Neil Armstrong landed on the moon, Norman studied the simulated lunar landscape at the manned space flight program of the Johnson Space Center in Houston, Texas. He drew the painting of the landing vehicle and astronaut in 1967, two years before the actual landing (Marling, *Norman Rockwell,* p. 145).

"can show . . . noticed" expressed to David H. Wood, director of the Norman Rockwell Museum, in Rome, 1976, in "Foreword," *Norman Rockwell: A Definitive Catalogue,* edited by Laurie Norton Moffat (Hanover and London: University Press New England, 1986).

"He never . . . beings." Christopher Finch, "Introduction," *102 Favorite Paintings by Norman Rockwell* (New York: Crown Publishers, Inc., 1978), p. 13.

SELECTED BIBLIOGRAPHY

Bolling, Landrum. "Norman Rockwell's Legacy." *Saturday Evening Post,* May/June 1994.

Durrett, Deanne. *The Importance of Norman Rockwell.* San Diego: Lucent Books, Inc., 1997.

Finch, Christopher. "Introduction." *102 Favorite Paintings by Norman Rockwell.* New York: Crown Publishers, Inc., 1978.

Guptill, Arthur L. *Norman Rockwell Illustrator.* New York: Ballantine Books, 1976.

Ingram, Scott, as told to Herschell Gordon Lewis. *Symbol of America: Norman Rockwell.* Huntingdon Valley, PA: Lynell Marketing, Inc., 1982.

Jarman, Rufus. "The Dickens of the Paintbrush." *New Yorker,* March 17, 1945.

Marling, Karol Ann. *Norman Rockwell.* New York: Harry N. Abrams, Inc., in association with the National Museum of Art, Smithsonian Institution, 1997.

Meyer, Susan E. *Norman Rockwell's People.* New York: Harry N. Abrams, Inc., 1981.

Moffatt, Laurie Norton, ed. *Norman Rockwell: A Definitive Catalogue.* 2 vols. Hanover and London: University Press of New England, 1986.

Rockwell, Norman. *Norman Rockwell: My Adventures as an Illustrator as Told to Thomas Rockwell.* Garden City, NY: Doubleday & Co., 1960.

Spalding, Don. Phone interview with Susan E. Meyer on audiotape, October 7, 1980. Norman Rockwell Museum, Stockbridge, MA.

Twain, Mark. *Adventures of Tom Sawyer.* Norwalk, CT: Easton Press, 1995.

Walton, Donald. *A Rockwell Portrait.* Kansas City, MO: Sheed Andrews & McMeel, Inc., 1978.

ILLUSTRATION CREDITS

p. iii *God Bless Us, Every One! Saturday Evening Post* cover, December 15, 1934. Oil on canvas, 55 x 31 inches. Courtesy of The Norman Rockwell Museum at Stockbridge (NRM).

p. vi *Triple Self-Portrait. Saturday Evening Post* cover, February 13, 1960. Oil on canvas, 44.5 x 34.25 inches. NRM

p. 2 Norman and Jarvis, c. 1896. NRM

p. 2 *The Champ. Saturday Evening Post* cover, April 29, 1922. Oil on canvas, whereabouts unknown. NRM

p. 3 Norman and a friend holding frogs, c. 1905. NRM

p. 3 The Rockwell family, c. 1904. NRM

p. 5 *No Swimming. Saturday Evening Post* cover, June 4, 1921. Oil on canvas, 25.25 x 22.25 inches. NRM

p. 6 Portrait of Norman Rockwell at Art Students League, undated. Peter A. Juley & Son, The Permanent Collection of the Art Students League of New York, c. 1912.

p. 7 George Bridgman's men's life class at the Art Students League of New York, after 1912. Unidentified photographer, The Permanent Collection of the Art Students League of New York.

p. 8 *Crackers in Bed.* Original oil for advertisement, Edison Mazda Lamp Works, 1920. 40 x 28 inches. Christie's, New York.

p. 11 *Norman with Wooden Case.* Illustration from *My Adventures as an Illustrator,* 1960. NRM

p. 13 *Joe with Dog Finds Man in Snow. Boys' Life* illustration, December, 1913. NRM

p. 15 *Salutation (Boy with Baby Carriage). Saturday Evening Post* cover, May 20, 1916. Oil on canvas, 20.75 x 18.625 inches. NRM

p. 16 *Pioneer of the Air. Saturday Evening Post* cover, July 23, 1927. 22.5 x 18.5 inches. NRM

p. 18 Norman and Mary, 1930. NRM

p. 18 Norman and Mary's three sons: Thomas, Jarvis, and Peter, c. 1940. NRM

p. 19 *My Studio Burns.* Illustration, *Saturday Evening Post* story, July 17, 1943. Charcoal on paper, 21 1/2 x 17 inches. NRM

p. 20 *Schoolmaster Flogging Tom Sawyer.* Illustration, *Adventures of Tom Sawyer,* 1936. Oil on canvas, 25 x 20 inches.

p. 21 *Tom and Becky in the Cave.* Illustration, *Adventures of Tom Sawyer,* 1936. Oil on canvas, 25 x 20 inches.

Illustrations by Norman Rockwell for *Adventures of Tom Sawyer* are reproduced with the permission of MBI, Inc. and are copyright 1936, c. 1964 by The Heritage Press and The Easton Press (MBI, Inc.), Norwalk, Connecticut, U.S.A.

p. 23 *Louisa May Alcott in Her Attic at Concord, Massachusetts.* Illustration, *Women's Home Companion*, December 1937. Unknown, presumed to be oil. NRM

p. 25 *Deadline. Saturday Evening Post* cover, October 8, 1938. Oil on canvas, 31 x 36 inches. NRM

p. 27 Norman using a balopticon to enlarge his drawing, c. 1949. NRM

p. 29 *The Gillis Heritage. Saturday Evening Post* cover, September 16, 1944. Oil on board, 13.25 and 10.625 inches. NRM

p. 30 *Rosie the Riveter.* Saturday Evening Post cover, May 29, 1943. Oil on canvas, 52 x 38.75. NRM

p. 31 *Four Freedoms* signing, Hecht's Department Store, Washington, D.C., April 1943. NRM

p. 33 *Freedom of Speech. Saturday Evening Post* story, February 20, 1943. Oil on canvas, 45.75 x 35.5 inches. NRM

p. 33 *Freedom of Worship. Saturday Evening Post* story, February 27, 1943. Oil on canvas, 46 x 35.5 inches. NRM

p. 33 *Freedom from Fear. Saturday Evening Post* story, March 13, 1943. Oil on canvas, 45.75 x 35.5 inches. NRM

p. 33 *Freedom from Want. Saturday Evening Post* story, March 6, 1943. Oil on canvas, 45.75 x 35.5 inches. NRM

p. 36 *Breaking Home Ties. Saturday Evening Post* cover, September 25, 1954. NRM

p. 37 *Girl at the Mirror. Saturday Evening Post* cover, March 6, 1954. Oil on canvas, 31.5 x 29.5 inches. NRM

p. 38 Norman and Molly, c. 1962. NRM

p. 39 The model for the April Fool painting. NRM

p. 40 *The Discovery. Saturday Evening Post* Christmas cover, 1956. Oil on canvas, 35.25 x 32.5 inches. NRM

p. 41 *April Fool: Girl with Shopkeeper. Saturday Evening Post* cover, April 3, 1948. Oil on canvas, 18 x 17 inches. NRM

p. 43 Rockwell at work painting the background for *Connoisseur,* 1962. Photographer: Louis Lamone. NRM

p. 44 *Connoisseur. Saturday Evening Post* cover, January 13, 1962. Oil on canvas, 37.75 x 31.5 inches. NRM

p. 45 Norman painting Abraham Lincoln, 1964. Photographer: Louis Lamone. NRM

p. 46 Norman painting *The Problem We All Live With,* 1963. Photographer: Louis Lamone. NRM

p. 48 *The Problem We All Live With. Look* illustration, January 14, 1964. Oil on canvas, 36 x 58 inches. NRM

p. 52 *Man on the Moon. Look* illustration, January 10, 1967. Oil on canvas, 63 7/8 x 40 1/8 inches. National Air and Space Museum, Smithsonian Institution, Washington, D.C.

INDEX